By Hand

By Hand
John Reibetanz

Brick Books

Library and Archives Canada Cataloguing in Publication

Title: By hand / John Reibetanz.
Names: Reibetanz, John, 1944– author.
Description: Poems.
Identifiers: Canadiana (print) 20189067691 | Canadiana (ebook) 20189067705 |
ISBN 9781771315036
   (softcover) | ISBN 9781771315050 (PDF) | ISBN 9781771315043 (EPUB)
Classification: LCC PS8585.E448 B94 2019 | DDC C811/.54—dc23

We acknowledge the Canada Council for the Arts, the Government of Canada
through the Canada Book Fund, and the Ontario Arts Council for their support
of our publishing program.

The author photo was taken by Timothy Reibetanz.
The book is set in Sabon.
The cover image is by Winit Peesuad.
Design and layout by Marijke Friesen.
Printed and bound by Coach House Printing.

Brick Books
431 Boler Road, Box 20081
London, Ontario N6K 4G6

www.brickbooks.ca

Humans are unusual in having special anatomy whose dominant role is the restructuring of the world around them, the hands.
    —Mike Hansell, *Bird Nests and Construction Behaviour*

Until modern times, apart from the esoteric knowledge of the priests, philosophers, and astronomers, the greater part of human thought and imagination flowed through the hands.... A creature who was clever enough to use the potential energy of a drawn bowstring to propel a small spear (arrow)...had reached a new level of thought.... Conceivably...the first use of a bow was as a musical instrument.... And yet the feathering of the arrow . . . was possibly due to a purely magical identification of the arrow with the wings of a living bird.
    —Lewis Mumford, *Technics and Human Development*

Sentience was never our private possession. We live immersed in intelligence, enveloped and informed by a creativity we cannot fathom.
    —David Abram, *Becoming Animal*

For Julie,
by heart

Contents

I

Instruments:
"special anatomy"

The Lighter

The moving part was a cookie-sized ship's wheel,
   eight spokes radiating like compass points
from a central hub, each capped with a handle
   my forefingers and thumbs steered by pinching.

Somebody must have tossed it out as garbage
   when the wheel no longer struck sparks inside
the cylinder it spun on. I salvaged it,
   fired up by its chrome gleam in a trash bin.

If I'd been raised in the country, my trophies
   might have been snail shells, birds' eggs, arrowheads,
but in my dresser's bottom drawer, dungarees
   hid clock parts, keys, a bent hood ornament,

and the lighter. Weekends, parents sleeping in,
   my fingers steered the polished, tube-hulled boat
through heavy flannel-blanket seas to beaches
   or snug coves breaking from dream-misted coasts,

landforms more solid with each turn of the wheel—
   as if, freed from bondage to tobacco,
it now ignited primal light and made real
   things out of imagination's spectres.

Decades passed before I learned that a *lighter*
   was also a vessel used to unload
and lighten larger ships with too deep a draught
   to dock in port. Which explains the floating

feeling that still rises from a pliant hand
    and spirals up through arm, shoulder, and neck
until the mind, buoyant once more, unburdened
    of its misty cargo, can rekindle.

Mantegna Perhaps

from the German of Durs Grünbein

Once in half-sleep   between grasp and give
I saw my hands   their jaundiced hide
that of a stranger   a corpse in a morgue.
At meals they wielded   knife and fork, tools
fit for the cannibal   knitting amnesia of
hunt, din, thunk.
                        The empty plate
of a palm rose up   plump hump of
the ultimate ape   who could grasp all
in a primate world.   Mantegna perhaps
might have foreshadowed   their horror unvarnished,
these fatty calluses.
                        What was the future
mapped in the handlines   its haps or mishaps
against the terror   of pores where sweat streamed
like the inward grasping   engraved on a brow.

Innermost Hand

from the German of Rainer Maria Rilke

Hand's intimate part. Sole that runs no more
but by feeling. That, facing upwards,
mirroring,
takes in heavenly streets, alike
wandering.
That has learned to scale water
when it scoops.
That springs from wells,
a shifter of every shape.
That steps into other hands,
turning its kind
into landscape:
wanders, arrives in them,
fills them with arrival.

Grooving

This music goes a long way back   before the needle
coasted in its groove on your grandfather's black vinyl
before the bow sang from valleys in the flexed saw blade

of his grandfather   before ancient breath fluted from
the vent-holes ancient tools notched in the small vaulted roof
of a hollow bone   back to where a flintstone burin

etched silent scales into softer stone   or to the beach
where a pointed fragment of shell gave the hand's airy
motions a home in driftwood   the way the waves in their

ins and outs hold the rhythm of the wind's breath   this hand
makes music with the world around it   but not without
an instrument   chisel or gouge to transpose the mind's

notations to the range of pith and grain   wood pushing
against the carver's flexed wrist   retorting   giving back
its own resonance to the tuning body   duet

of earthbound songsters that becomes a trio when   long
after the woodshed stills   you run your finger over
the carving   thrill to the flutings   and you're in the groove

Hands

1. Roucadour Cave, 28000 BCE

A finger of flame trembles on the juniper sprig
as the sandstone lamp's tallow puddle shrinks   the finger
will not point for long   but she does not need long   the red-

spotted aurochs flank already dry as the flank of
rock-wall it gallops into   only the homage now
to honour the wall   blowing red spots around her hand's

flat branching trunk   leaving its white spirit wedded to
the cave whose breath never flees   as will hers   following
morning flower-breath's mist on blue petals   or breath-clouds

rising from an aurochs at hunt's end   or the drawing
in and out of her unpainted hand to shift the lamp
along the floor as she raises and lowers the bone

tube through which her breath reddens the wall   not with her blood
for it will also flee   but with earth's blood   the stone vein
she rooted out   ground to powder and made flow again

from her mouth   so that in return for her gift of pulse
the cave body will   as it holds song after song leaves
her lips   hold up for other flickering lights the hand

that carved the lamp   and that made the dead aurochs' stilled hooves
charge again   as they do long after the last aurochs
has left and this hand's work is our only hold on it

2. Palaikastro, Crete, 1500 BCE

Painstaking and prone to pain because mortal   his quick
fingers have twisted the tiny bronze awl   one way first
then in reverse   thousands of times in what we call *clock-*

wise and *counter-clockwise* turns   drilling holes into eight
separate ivory parts for olivewood dowels
to link the god's limbs   but neither his head nor his god's

knows *clock*   the god timing his comings and goings with
a hoe's blade or a scythe's   the carver sharpening *now*
to a point finer than a clepsydra's thinning drop   to pierce

the shell of hours and days and speed Orion's image
into eternity   for nothing earthly can be
worthy of a god   so the same hand that coaxed tendon

vein and knucklebone from an ivory stump will veil
the god's limbs in gold leaf   placing the pale muscled foot
on a spangled plinth whose unfathomable waters

hold the night sky's infinities   though another hand
in times of later gods   to please them   will rip this god
from his shrine   smash the golden-cloched head and carbonize

dismembered ivory   in flames whose earthbound ashes
a secular age will water-sieve to recover
and piece together sandal strap and foot   lobe and ear

finger and nail   not to placate a god flickering
in the light of long-extinct stars   but to pay homage
to ephemeral flesh and its fragile handiwork

3. Paris, 1927 CE

Bony and restless   Cocteau's hands are two crabs whose paths
cross for a moment   how can Berenice Abbott capture
no not capture   blink her shutter at their now before

now scuttles to then   first step   arrange them on his hat
see them as birds alighting on a round felt nest   but
one whose downy brim and ridged crown shimmer with their own

winged motion   next step   widen the aperture so light's
arrow pierces only at the focus   scattering
all but his hands to haze   the shawl of their skin speckled

with pores and thin as a lizard's   barely protecting
the raised veins' rippling lifelines   wispy as vanishing
instants whose sole fitting mementos can never be

monumental   but must hover in suspension like
speeches Cocteau fabricates to cup for a twinkling
the fireflies of his actors' breath   or like the light-

loving silver halides dancing in the emulsion
Abbott's hands will prepare   those hands out of the picture
as   she well knows   women's have always been   but working

behind the scenes   not to hold in stone what has died or
in gold what was never born   but one with living earth
practicing in borrowed light the art of breath and blink

II

Visions:
"magical identification"

Found in Translation

Two long-stemmed roses nuzzle, one tousled
petal-head resting on another, in
a carving titled *Pár*, Hungarian
word sounding too much like the English *pair*
    to be translated into something else.

In this case irresistible, the wood
coming from a Hungarian *pear* tree:
the homophone proclaims a match between
subject and substance, an artist's vision
    easily taking root in solid ground.

Yet, not so easy: linguists in the know
know *pár* translates more truly as *lovers*.
Yet again, the mystery that converts
pairs to lovers is not so far removed
    from art that turns a pear's wood into roses.

The Roses, XVI

from the French of Rainer Maria Rilke

Let's not talk about you, ineffable
being your nature.
Other flowers grace the table
that you transfigure.

Place you in a simple vase—
and look how everything changes:
it's perchance the same phrase,
but chanted by an angel.

Flight Plans

Apollo doesn't get it,
e.g. the god's hissy fit
pitched when Marsyas's flute
outsang his immortal lute,
and payback for fine playing
was that poor satyr's flaying.

Here his hand, reaching to catch
a bit of maidenly snatch,
is met with Daphne's rough bark
instead of her thigh's theme-park:
shock, at finding the door so
shut, shudders through his torso,

while Bernini's having fun
at the god's consternation
by sculpting two little stones
which look like lost *cojones*
on the ground beside his heel
as divine toe bumps tree-bole,

and by hinting Apollo
is unable to follow
the laurel's evolution
through one more substitution.
Daphne's fingers, grown thinner
than mere leaves, will begin her

career in the air. Feathered
(and not, as he thinks, tethered)
and launched from the tree trunk's pad,
not sad, never to be had
by him, with full throat she sings,
her spread branches turned to wings.

The Barovier Wedding Cup, 1450

Ping the rim with your fingernail:
the goblet's upturned bell will ring
in some small imagined Venice—
crystal-walled, glassed in like the scene
glimpsed through a snow globe's glittering.

No hint of winter here: grasses
green the fields where courtiers' horses
under cloudless vaulting cobalt
canter towards a fountain splashing
gold over maidens' uncloaked flesh.

Angelo Barovier began
with river pebbles ground to brown
dust, then furnace-scoured to crystal,
every dash of darkness vanquished
by soda ash's plumed phoenix.

With rounds of breath the glass-blower
shaped the sphere of a glass flower,
his steady hand enamelling
the curved sweep of its petal-ring
into a wood's sunswept clearing.

It is the Venice of his dreams,
gold stars afloat in lapis dome,
the sea tamed to gold curlicues
of foam, and in between, acres
of solid ground where downy streams

feather from hidden headwaters
that never were. Storm waves salted
the real Venice's wells, salt loam
stunted flowers and tarnished domes,
fog dimmed its phoenixes to gulls.

Somewhere since 1450, names
of the gentleman and his dame
whose portraits frame the dreamy scene
spilled from memory's cup. Known drained
into unknown, settled again

among pebbled silt. The last horse
trotted past a canalled concourse
four hundred years ago. Trembling,
some future hand may make this bell's
last ring a shattering of glass.

For now, two figures, one in red,
one in a grey brocade, riding
lithe ponies, lead the small parade.
They may lead you to see, in grey,
the salt and ash that clarified

the dim Venetian dust; in red,
imagination's heady must
transforming brines to vintages;
and in the drained, upturned crystal
no bell, but a domed marriage bed.

Tilman Riemenschneider's Hands

play silent music to the mind's cupped ear   a dirge here
as the apostles in his altarpiece of the Last
Supper catch the refrain   that one of them has sold out

their leader   from their light-grained limewood hands you'd think them
disciples of Chopin not of Christ   long thin digits
for bridging the octaves of nocturnes on instruments

uninvented in 1504   look how the splayed
fourth and fifth fingers of this seated figure betray
the strain as if stretched on a rack   how his third finger

presses his robe's unyielding fabric   how Saint Philip's
thumb and forefinger mime a pistol he might raise at
the upright Judas whose fist bulges with the muscles

closing around a money bag   but most of all how
hands wreathe the sleeping head of John   his hands a pillow
plumped under his cheek   Christ's left hand a lullaby draped

over his shoulder   all their faces uncreased as if
they shared his dream's happy ending   where a new heaven
attunes its harps   not where the nightmare trumpets bellow

and hooves crush   as they would in the Peasants' Revolt when
the triumphant Prince-Bishop of Würzburg's instruments
played on the carver Riemenschneider's hands   and broke them

Decipherings

Both kinds of reading meant tracing lines with her finger
at first   until the eye grew adept at pivoting
over ridge and groove without handholds   the outdoor kind

came sooner though harder   probing the shifting cliffside's
dark rows of shale   questions tapped by her small pick would go
unheard under the sea's hammering   yet bring to light

a cryptic alphabet of bone and tooth   whose meaning
remained dark long after the incoming tide erased
the scribbles of her shoes from the sand   the indoor kind

opened easily as reflected candlelight streamed
off the gold margins of the pages   her hand meeting
the hands that *formed the dry land*   vast fingers rising from

the letters to knead brown doughy earth   or embed trees
in the Garden like candles in a cake   did their grip
pull down the spooled-up snakes the tide unveiled   or squeeze them

to stone for punishment   giving their hiss to the sea
and did His palms press her first bound find   crocodile-flat
skull   round eye sockets fused to a snout so long it took

days for her needle and brush to expose the nearly
two hundred teeth   brow and beak like a wicked giant's
scissors   here comes a chopper to chop off your head   hers

turned   wary   to the delicate lattice her next find
traced in the marl   harp strings   or harpist's fine finger bones
tines of a lady's ivory comb   which all proved linked

together as if glued to prevent any motion
but a single quick flipper-thrust towards prey awaited
by rows of conical teeth still sharp enough to draw

blood from her touch   and a sense she might never construe
the lines that joined   *Hath not my hand made all these things?*   to
these smothered primordial creatures grown out of hand

The Dresden Angel

Bowing slightly, as in polite concern
while offering a chair to someone old
and weary, she gestures with her left arm
to where chairs might be if mere light could hold

furniture; but she leans from a tower,
no upholstery in sight, not even
a chip of wood, and on the distant ground
stones shadow the dust of firebombed Dresden.

Sandstone herself, some call her Dame Kindness
but only an angel could have survived
the furnace blast that pressed spread wings into
a cape around her shoulders and splintered

her neighbour-statue, Wisdom. An angel,
yet not immune to human ills, the thumb
she shared with us sheared off. Her fingers
cannot grasp—nor can her mind, dumbfounded,

unless the broad composure of her face
means she is not deranged but blind, those eyes
seared in a flash to stone and now tearless
while overlooking rows of blank facades

whose eye-cases once glittered back the flames
before their watery lenses dried up.
Better to be blind than see the roofless
stone as her mortal kind, skulls blown open.

Earthbound

1. Donatello, *Madonna of the Clouds*

Like an armchair, Mary's solid legs
cradle him. Her left hand's tensed fingers
dimple his shoulder, while her right arm hugs
the place a spear will pierce the grown infant.

Chairless she sits, not on some riverbank
but in a cirrus stream, the overlapping waves
of cloud one with the ripples of her woven
robe: miracle fabric, air-spun, sheer heaven.

Still finer ripples in the stone reveal
she bends a troubled brow over her child,
as if her eyes saw the invisible

and witnessed that a seeming-solid heart,
like clouds by lightning, can be cleft apart
by arrows from sheer spirit's arsenal.

2. Donatello, *The Martyrdom of St. Sebastian*

Arrows, an arrow's length from their target,
threaten from stretched bowstrings. At point-blank range
how can they miss? Four shafts have already
skewered his torso, pointed tips emerging

from his back like mechanical extensions
of the marksmen's taut bronze arms, punching through
the bars of his ribcage, a strict horizon line
cleaving the relief's compressed world in two.

Ranged above the split, all hands are fists—
the shooters clasp bows, Sebastian's right hand clenches
in pain—except for the angel's palm, raised in peace,

a sign the ape-browed marksmen cannot see,
like the two halos touching like twin suns
or the angel's robe, wind-rippled from his descent.

3. Péter Cserháti, *Gratitude, 1969*

You see that figure at the bronze sphere's base,
down on his knees, bent over, elbows
and clasped hands hugging the ground: has he been beaten?
Or, wombed in that sphere, is he about to be born?

What are the layered bands above and behind him?
Waves of an old world that nearly drowned him?
Or, floating in clouds, the sun-bathed horizon
of a new world whose shore he's landed on?

Why try to circle with bronze a fugitive moment?
Because bronze will endure and will not let
this day's light drain into memory's thirsty sand.

A circle because he, wombed in gratitude, senses
at moments like this a perfection that surrounds
the incomplete orbits that mark our questions.

4. Péter Cserháti, *Motherhood, Latina, 1969*

The image could be from a Renaissance tondo,
Mother and Child by Michelangelo
or Botticelli: close-up on infant's head
and mother's breast, twinned rounds within this round.

Yet, this scene is drawn from life. Real motherhood,
not couched in some idealized verdant landscape:
winter, a postwar Italian camp's
barracks crammed with exhausted refugees.

And yet again—the flight from oppression,
the miracle of birth in barren December—
real present takes the shape of storied past

and comforts, hinting that beyond this vision
a new world's unimaginable future
will unfold from this infant's rounded fist.

Carving a New Creation

Hush say the waves   hush hush   an orbed miracle hovers
        a rim of dawn crowning the flat world's edge   rises from
a sunbather's body level as the sand   but for

the promontory of her raised left leg   the shadowed
        cave mouth under the small of her back   and this soft sphere
of breast   inviting touch like a Buddha's open palm

benign incarnate sun   this will not burn the other
        bathers sheltered from an ancient sky god's glare under
the rib-studded shields of beach umbrellas   this roundness

no saint's head fringed with gold   but aureoled where shading
        hints of the areola's rosy bloom   flower whose
petalled trumpet has no need for the breath of angels

Lotte Reiniger's Magic Shadows

You couldn't call them scissors in her hands   if the clashed
swords of scissors slash and shear   her blades whispered through a void
of thick black paper   their strokings calling up paddlers

and plodders   gallopers and swoopers   spelling lions
from mane-shaped cursive sweeps   Baghdad minarets from strips
of lacy trim   and Cinderella's poverty from

a ragged hem   her art not merely deft fingerwork
but transmigration of souls   her own into stone rounds
of tracery or the muscular vertical of

an eagle taking wing   and the beholder's into
a genesis that turned tapered shadows to rosy
flesh of thigh and flank   grey stripes to sunlight   and the gap

between pose and pose to limbs in action   while she fled
the Nazis' impenetrable shade   the stick figures
pushed into ovens   the metal silhouettes of tanks

treading Aladdin's sands   her most moving creations
weightless not with absence but with the magical flights
of bodies wholly grounded in the passage of light.

The Installation

The Della Robbia kiln fired up with orders from
guilds of silk weavers and metal workers, furriers
and skinners, finishers of foreign cloth, requesting

swirling-robed Resurrections, cradling-armed Madonnas,
leaf-loined Adams and Eves, and Sacred Conversations
on cloudpuffs between saints and the Holy Family—

but this Nativity speaks to the universal
commonality of clay, from the marl Luca scooped
out of the Arno's bed to the light-quickened humus

of the eyes that, for hundreds of years, have read the notes
inscribed on the banner an angel is unscrolling
over the heads of adoring mother, surrogate

father, and hay-couched infant, whose hand lifts a blessing
next to the snout of the donkey with eyes closed like those
of Saint Teresa in ecstasy as he nibbles

divine straw that, like donkey, ox, humans, and angels
conceals its clay under a glassy veil of colour,
the family hallmark of the Della Robbia

reminding us—as any relief does, even if
we join the chorus in *Gloria* above this stall—
of the unfinished beyond the reach of hand or eye

III

Fingerings:
"a drawn bowstring"

Strung

from the German of Paul Celan

Near the hailstone, in
the blighted corn-
cob, at home, in
fealty to the late, hard
November stars:

in the heartstitch
knit from wormspeech:

a string, from which
your dartscript whizzes,
marksman.

Dickinson's Envelopes

She needs containers that will not contain   but like in-
verted pockets   hold all outside in their insides   pen-
ning nothing in   her window offers instances   as

heading from left to right   across the field of vision
each squirrel's tail prints a quotation mark   that opens
on an endless moving line   or in the garden   how

pouring upwards from green funnels   at ankle level
lily of the valley's pea-sized bells   discharge volleys
that echo through far nostrils   or from the forest floor

a mushroom's brown unfurlment concentrates   the whole round
earth beneath it   so her creations begin with light
liberated from folds of darkness   as she scissors

the envelopes' sealed hollows into shores   each sloped edge
a beachhead on infinity   the grained beige margins
broadened by jetties of print   like flower beds enlarged

through division   vacancies further claimed by hyphen's
reach   and apostrophe's curved grasp   yet never a claim
staked   in this ground too paper-thin for rooted sureness

no settlements of ink   but penciled tents   their fabric
a weave reversible   spun of such gossamer thread
as to be one   at night   with the canopy of stars

Thoreau's Pencils

All change is a miracle to contemplate   he writes
contemplating the pond's daily miracles   how ice
forms in winter   first printing the surface with crystal

leaves   as if it flowed into moulds pressed on the liquid
mirror by the veined hands of waterplants   and he writes
of bubbles   clear bubbles honeycombing surface ice

in spring   sun turning each to a burning-glass that melts
thick shards beneath   or dark bubbles of frogspawn sprouting
tails and light-catching eyes   he writes in pencil because

making pencils is the family livelihood   and
because bubbles of ink dry unchangeable   staining
the paper's fibres into mourning   while the oar-strokes

of a pencil leave no trace on the freshened surface
when wind-smoothed by an eraser's sweeps   and where pens seek
the icy might of swords   the pencil takes a meek course

yielding line by line   every sharpened point a whittling
down   yet every glossy-barked cedar shaft liveliest
at its core   the graphite that can carry thought from mind

through hand to paper   a heartwood most unbreakable
he discovers   when mixed as we are   with clay   *Am I*
he writes   *not partly leaves and vegetable mould myself?*

"Bird's Nest" Hunt

Turned-in toes   glass ankles   matchstick calves   legs failing him
from the outset   he learned to rely instead on thumb

and finger to walk a brush   and touch white fields with bloom
like Spring's footsteps   lilac traces   yellow trails of lime

his hand   Ruskin wrote   *always more sensitive than firm*
his eye too easily spooked by speed to hold its aim

at a stream's leaps or the twitches of birds   but supreme
in the unlifting mist on grape clusters   the pooled gleam

of still-life vase and oyster shell   earning his nickname
by miming the fixed intricate visual rhythm

transcribed by chaffinch and sparrow in the medium
of twig   moss   and feather   and their held round notes of cream

and hyacinth   the artist himself a great ovum
round-shouldered bundle wheelbarrowed with sketchpad through farm

and wood   his brush   re-threading loops of a woven home
finds   in each white-streaked blue dome   flight's embryonic dream

In Touch

Both hand and voice belonged to the same body, and the same sensibility
set them in motion. — Durs Grünbein

When her mother was her age, the way you waved *goodbye*
and keep in touch was holding your closed hand tucked against
your cheek, fingers clenched around the imaginary

handset, but now she raises two fists as if ready
to parry a blow, except that she's giving the *thumbs-*
up sign—not to spare some revenant gladiator

but to press intended keypad letters, those junctions
where thumbs meet marks an ancient stylus pressed into clay
when it joined sounds a voice made in an ancient language

to eyes and throats centuries away, as she will join
her printed voice-tracks to the lines reaching up and down
through time, left and right through space, like the meshwork of wires

and pipes running underneath a city—this city
of shared life, sprawling beyond boundaries of land or
body, pressing out *tears* or making her LOL.

Fingers and Thumbs

Sometimes the moment issues from patience   like water
from rockface   so he waits out gusts bending the cedar's
fingers of frond and blocking the red tricycle seat

he needs to anchor the middle distance   while a still
more patient window vigil will outstay morning clouds
that flicker his unbroken light   and sometimes it takes

the grip of memory to hold a yellow birch leaf
spinning in mid-air   or a jogger's foot glimpsed between
fence slats   lifted aloft   but always it's the pinch of

finger and thumb on his brush that keeps them from coming
to grief   keeps the half-closed garage door across the street
ajar with promise   yet later in the afternoon

changing light calls him out to the garden   where the same
finger and thumb that caressed one another sowing
spring seed   will meet like teeth to deadhead roses or crush

leaf-thin green shells of aphids   and in that unroofed room
he'll see how his shadow defines itself by breaking
the shaft of sun   feel his lungs make life by taking in

what the wind offers   and be content with artless time
until   tacking up the fingerpainting his daughter
brings home from school   he follows the brittle labyrinth

of her thumbprint   purple on a leaf of stiff paper
already starting to buckle under the dried paint
and knows   come morning   he'll be once more at his easel.

The Zeeland Tapestries

get so much wrong   those four fireships lobbed on an ebb tide
into the Spanish fleet weren't launched until a week
after Lieven Keersemaecker's attack   depicted

in the same frame   while the foray bathed in smoke-hazed sun
at the edge of the Zierikzee tapestry   took place
one night before the breached palisade at its centre

was breached   but you can't blame the weavers for deleting
a Catholic church from Middelburg   or a citadel
from Flushing   years before the victorious rebels

razed both   for the weavers were postwar refugees   new
to Zeeland   witnessing naval battles through a lens
clouded with the smoke of two decades of memory's

retreats and forced advances   and sat facing the wrong
side of each hanging as they worked from mirror-image
cartoons   drawn from designs from sketches pieced together

from tattered charts and recollections   their handiwork
itself a piecemeal stitching of bright silk strands of weft
into colourless warp   where the cut and knotted threads'

confusion brought them closer than the finished side's sheen
to a sea laced with blood and spangled with bodies
and limbs   closer than anyone wanted to be to

the cannonball that   bouncing off waves like a skipped stone
flew through Admiral Jan de Moor's cabin and blew him
apart   or to the wood splinter that shattered the eye

of Admiral de Boisot   who now looks out at us
clear-eyed and resplendent as   spotless in gold brocade
he leads the charge   his wound woven whole by the fingers

of healers who knew that history isn't rightly
what happened   but a fabric whose waves dance in the sun
beneath ships where pain tapers to a spill of red silk.

Confinements

1.

Or through imagining of a wasted life   or two
the first survives in the glossy coating on a square
of paper one-hundredth of an inch thick   my mother's

Uncle Joey   whose raised left hand covers his bald head
in a gesture half salute   half mock astonishment
at which his brother Chris   younger only in years   casts

a disapproving sidewards glance   I am absent from
the photo   my ten-year-old thumb pressing the button
that stores it in my Brownie Hawkeye   Uncle Joey's

right hand holds a knitted beret   harvest of that week's
Occupational Therapy   the brothers stand on
the stone front steps of the state hospital where Joey's

body lives   his mind on holiday elsewhere   I had
never met him before that afternoon   would never
meet him again   but he might have met the occupant

of a second wasted life   who spent most of it in
the same fenced place   Lawrence Mocha   a fellow patient
whose OT needed tools larger than knitting needles

to scoop out graves in the hospital cemetery
I like to think of the two men sharing a dinner
in the refectory   of Joey   who could never

hold onto anything   giving Lawrence a beret
to keep the sun off his head   but perhaps they only
met after Lawrence's hands positioned the wood frame

and his foot levered a spade beside and beneath it
in the meadow they share now   free of stones or markers
where the ragweed and common yarrow spread unconfined

2.

Beneath an English garden oyster shells share the soil
with Roman coins   brooches   and an intact mosaic
none complain   the shells have known nothing but confinement

since before they were carted from the coast in barrels
of salt water   the medallions circulate among
earthworms   and the polished stones keep their glaze even in

the absence of sun   how is it that simple compounds
of calcium or carbon fare better on their own
than a brainchild at the top of creation's ladder

like Genie   kept solitary from toddler to teen
strapped in a potty chair all day   paddled for prattling
whose rescuers could teach her only isolated

words   splinters of mosaic   the sentences she might
have spoken entombed in the catacombs of her brain
leg muscles so cramped she half-crouched   hands held rabbit-style

in front as if set to play some spectral piano
hands that in the absence of shaped breath became her voice
urging a crayon through thought-halls   drawing connections

from stick figures to spinning hoops   imagine the *brown*
green and *red*   three of the twenty words she knew when found
after staring her whole life at plastic rain gear hooked

on the wall across from her chair   colours bloom from her
hand like geraniums from a Roman child's stone tomb
repurposed as planter beneath an English window

Keys for the Homeless

This Alice   lacking a wonderland   will keep the keys
to apartments for the soul   finger them on the propped
legless trunk of a piano   and turn them over

rent-free to three hundred tenants camping every week
on wooden benches from which   forbidden to leave   they
rise to explore Chopin's rooms   the key of C minor

opens 10/12   where all their upheavals are played out
jackbooted troopers mimed by a left-hand rampage through
the piano's basement   screams of the displaced transposed

into the right hand's cross-rhythmed refusal to turn
itself into blunt instrument or paw   insistence
persisting even through the final forced march down to

oblivion   pain made nearly bearable by the
fingers that   tensed and cramped from splitting mica all day
in a dank work-hut   flutter over the ivories

like moths night has released from torpor   spread wings climbing
untrammeled through the low ceiling to 25/1
where the key of A flat major unlocks a room filled

with waves unfurling from an unseen harp steadily
as from a heart's strong tide   to lift souls up from human
bodies into the only earthly home they will know.

Song

from the German of Paul Celan

Marked by chance, the auguries unwindblown,
the numbers multiplied, unfairly blossomswept,
the Lord a raining near-fugitive who looks on
as lies sevenfold
                kindle, knives
                                butter up, crutches
break into perjury, U-
under
        this
                world
the nullth already roots,
                        lion,
sing you the folksong
of tooth and soul, both
rock.

IV

Earth Tones:
"immersed"

Sonnets to Orpheus, 2:14

from the German of Rainer Maria Rilke

Look at these flowers, loyal to the earthly,
to whom we on the brink of fate lend fate—
but who *knows* that! If they regret withering,
it is our lot to *be* their regret.

All things want to float. Yet we move heavy with doom,
loading our selves on everything, by gravity enraptured.
For things, oh, we are withering teachers,
while in them eternal childhood blooms.

If someone took them into his innermost sleep
and slept deeply with things, oh how lightly he'd rise
renewed for the new day, up from their shared deeps.

Or maybe he'd stay, and they would bloom and praise
him, the convert, now like one of their own,
all become siblings, hushed in the winds of the meadows.

Beyond Grasp

They begin in hand to hand combat   the man-hand's thumb
and fingers locked around the bow saw's haft   easily
wrestling the leaf-hands to the ground though far outnumbered

by those fine-lobed butterfly-thin flappers   hangers-on
that crash down shuddering with the felled limbs they cling to
as the row of pointed teeth chews straits through the ringed grain

and once the carver's hands have clamped the plank to his bench
the attack begins afresh   mallet and chisel slash
hunks and chips from the pinioned timber   but what those tensed

fingers search for cannot be found in the most deeply
cached heartwood   haunting instead the carver's mind   reverse
ghost   yet to come to life as pared stem   bevelled leaf-edge

and burnished petal   the tree sacrificed to turn its pith
from keelboard to rigging   undergrooved ripples swelling
as with a breath to take the shape of the dreamt blossoms

and though this posy will never sway in wind or draw
bees in with nectar   it will not draw into itself
in death   unwilting bouquet for which he turns thumbs down

on what pulses and passes   manhandling the pale wood
into which he carves his fear and ours   deeper pallor
than the most tightly folded flower or clenched fist can hold

Needlework from the English Civil War

I.

black ink the only thread   drawn into the paper with
the tip of a needle or seamstress's pin   thinner

than any quill point   and thus more thrifty   black because
the stitches of time are so often woven of loss

the Archbishop beheaded   mr dod and Goodwife
Liechfield dead   and Mr Quarles the poet   all within

two neighbouring three-inch frames   but also black because
only the cloth reverse knows all the colours in His

truestitch   we see through the fabric darkly   our weavings
all aranwork   of aranea the swart spider

cobwebbed and cobbled together   we longer retain
things taken from us than given   Lord pardon our un-

thankfulness   for the raising of Banbury Siege   Bess
Bamford's marriage   the King's rescue from Oxford   and red

satin   in the very same two frames   truth not something
that unrolls before us as a skein or seamless scroll

but must be worked   with myriads of tiny stitches
its mingled yarn evident even in ink's frozen

2.

confluences   where stars   ciphers   twined involutions
of freestanding capitals   inscribe how the past swirls

through and overruns the present   ravellings of ink
fountaining like the red stripes on Holofernes' neck

from the patterned legend of Judith embroidered by
Elizabeth's sister Judith   to the plain story

her needle never traced   of a King brought to the block
in some space beyond the paper's edge   frameless and blank

beyond stitching   beyond reach of simples flourishing
in bordered gardens   the rooted one at her back door

or the wrought one never watered yet sempervirens
spreading from the feet of her silken Adam and Eve

Transparencies

The layered whoness of this photograph includes both
seen and unseen   a cast of posers overflowing
Julia Cameron's frame   bearing witness to her sense

that the selves we wear for the world's lens bare only part
of our heartland   so her husband Charles   whom Goneril
might have called *milk-livered*   here commands the stage as Lear

in profile   lips pursed above snowy beard   right eye iced
with a contempt that lurked unguessed in Charles for the first
seventy-eight years of his life   until it froze out

Cordelia who   embodied here by Alice Liddell
has already lost her focus   vague grey eyes staring
through the fogged looking glass of a childhood left behind

while her sisters   Alice's as Cordelia's   sharpen
behind Lear's back   one of them pointing a gemmed finger
to his robe   whose beaded edge leads down to the photo's

centre where clawlike fingers ring a sceptre   their grasp
appropriately strong for Charles whose grip on life out-
lasted that of Alice's sister   and of Julia's

own daughter   also a Julia   dead the year after
her mother toned this albumen silver print with gold
chloride   then washed her black-stained hands with potassium

cyanide   risking the life the print outlived passing
into the hands of Maurice Sendak   who looked through walls
to the jungles lurking within them   who as a child

saw wild things in the wide bloodshot eyes of Holocaust-
surviving aunts and uncles   and who as an adult
envisioned a world where the wolf gives up the sceptre.

Three by Grinling Gibbons

for Bert Almon

1. The Cosimo Panel, 1682

Unearthly   a rectangular moon   the carving floats
moon-pale   its limewood like the ghost of wood   its craters
and mountains no cosmic roughcast   but lithely hand-rubbed

hollows and rondures   that resolve on close look into
a world of artful partnerings   quiver with arrows
sceptre with crown   palette with brushes   encircled by

a roundelay of fruits and flowers   and surmounted
by two perching doves linked bill to bill   all suspended
like a clockface frozen at a moment   in orbit

around paired autographs   letter-haloed medallion
of the painter Pietro da Cortona   and ribbon
unfurling Gibbons' engraved signature   these twin stars

in a galaxy where artists play sun-kings and seem
as untroubled as Louis himself by shadow   deep
undercutting that makes the roses only appear

to escape the Earth's pull   twin doves forever flightless
even if brought to life   because each one's unseen wing
remains uncarved   missing like the blossom-cups of sun

that rose from a once-living linden tree now hosting
no nectar-quickened bees but wooden grapes   forget-me-nots
that have forgotten tint and scent   and fruitless walnuts

beneath a tilted crown no hand can right   a sword hilt
whose blade of pure surmise lacks edge   a woodwind from whose
wood-clogged throat no song can break the unearthly silence.

2. The Modena Panel, 1685

Earthed too soon after being birthed   the shade of Gibbons'
infant son weighs down this carving   where three limp doves hang
by bound feet   dangling wings splayed like windblown umbrellas

downy hatchling nestled vainly between tall fledged birds
eyes of all three blank as cloth buttons   peapod and egg
cracked open below them   gravity's pitch at full tilt

in an ensemble less arrangement than debris field
from a fallen asteroid   but for its central group
of skull   medallion   and open music book   the skull

draped with a leaf-braid threaded by a quill pen whose nib
runs through the last link of a forged bronze chain suspending
the medallion portrait of the wigged carver himself

its oval echoing the eye socket of the skull
whose upper jawbone clasps a music book unfolding
the etched score and lyrics of this dirge by James Shirley

The glories of our blood and state Are shadows, not sub-
stantial things; There is no armour against fate; Death lays
his icy hand on kings. Sceptre and crown Must tumble

down, And in the dust be equal made With the poor crook-
ed scythe and spade.   Nothing in the panel's centre lifts
against the downbeat of the skull's grave song   but   almost

hidden by wrinkled fruit and broken shells at both ends
thin whorls of acanthus   each a little galaxy
of seed heads   spiral upwards like reversed waterfalls.

3. Overmantel, the Hampton Court Withdrawing Room, 1699

Like an acanthus whorl   this overmantel surrounds
blank space   but fills with portraits or mirrors where faces
come and go   while an acanthus holds only the play

of light and shade from passing days   except for the two
acanthus garlands here on either side   each serving
as perch and canopy for a pair of singing birds

you know are singing   not just because full throats tilt back
their open-beaked heads   but because the ripeness
of their trilling echoes through the apples and peaches

above and below them   the O of each acanthus
itself a mouth singing out the songbirds   whose lyrics
are the sun's as it marshals the shadows to raise up

these birds' tufted crowns in a daily round   an orbit
of music travelling at the speed of light   and pitched
so high it escapes the ear's whorled shell   o little birds

the long westward movement of your silent serenade
enfolds darkness   making requiem an overture
to birth   since the hand that carved you   now still and whitened

moved   when it could move   to carve away the heaviness
of rooted monumental sorrow   and leave only
these wispy portals for tides of light to ebb and flow

drawn not by an icy white stone in the black-creped sky
but by Earth's own circling   constantly carving its rounds
into ripening grapes and crowns of linden blossom.

Woodborne

What holds her up? asks Alfredo   the operatic
sweep of his arm appropriate for a man who spends
evenings away from his shop filling out the chorus

at La Fenice   but you can't tell whether the *she*
he means is all of Venice or the Virgin Mary
wafting heavenwards in the downsized Titian copy

he has framed for you   it turns out *wood* answers to both
Vergine and Serenissima   the city not
afloat or resting on cut stones whose reflections plunge

into the canals   but founded on sunken tree trunks
the lady whose red dress billows from her blue cape not
sailing on cherubs' mothlike wings   but (Alfredo's joke)

kept from shipwreck by the gilded wood he's braced around
her canvas   yet when the framer's forehead lifts into
ripples like the motorboat wakes that fret his lagoon

you know he shares the floating city's serious need
for woodgrain's unshifting waves   not only the water-
tight rings of larch pilings   but cirmolo's deep embrace

of the gold leaf he burnishes into its surface
according to the rules of Cennino Cennini's
Libro dell'Arte   Alfredo's bible   whose pages

were pressed from fourteenth-century wood pulp   and whose text
calls for instruments likewise rooted   his burnisher
the tooth of dog or wolf or leopard who roamed the woods

when trees were the sole cathedrals   the creatures of earth
flesh-feeding animals whose heaven was the forest
the gold-winged frame no phoenix   its brightness all leafage.

One Leaf

Életemnek claims the inscription on the flip side
of this cupped leaf   *my life* chiselled in Hungarian
into the flat base   where leafspread ends in a heartshape

wishful thinking if *my* life means the leaf's   none could last
the long decades since this was carved   the reddest-blooded
maple trembling for a few warm months before dropping

to cold   and if *my* is the carver's own testament
scored in hardwood   a palmate psalm praising the like flow
of life through veins of hand and leaf   this tonewood's solo

also carries a sombre theme in the dry leaving
of its rigid silence   but if *my life* means the one
whose 23 was grooved above it as an offshoot

when the wood came to leaf for her birthday   their love makes
my life shared   insisting that an unseen flood tide moves
more surely than a chisel through confines that divide

life from life   and life from leaf   reminding that the air
we coast on is one endless sea of breath   currents of
leaf-breath freshening the shores where human lips drink life

and leaves reach out to catch the drift of human whispers
whose breath drawn in by leaf-mouth will   when breathed out quickened
with sunlight   renew the maple's red in our hearts' blood

Leaf Morphs

The basic form possesses the capacity for endless modifications, whereby manifoldness is created out of unity. — Goethe, *Metamorphosis of Plants*

From her window
the child sees leaves as child-hands   in summer they applaud
themselves with every breeze   but in autumn   all grown up
their audience of birds flown   they blush and fall silent.

In winter the skittering fingers of musicians
stroking sonatas along the iced ground are one with
the fingers of writers inscribing runes on heaped snow.

Above them the bare trees flail and fling their arms across
each other on the sky's grey bed   tossing in their sleep
and when the sheets change to blue   all dream the same green dream.

In her album
as she pastes the sycamore leaf to the thick paper
        it is an infant in a green snowsuit   its peaked hood
                poking from a wedge of swaddling   the next page changes

                green to the mittened fingers of a sassafras leaf
                playing in late winter winds   in turn growing into
                a pin oak's Boy Scout salute   thumb holding pinky bent

beneath three pointed fingers   which on the page's flip-
                side become the upraised hand of an oath-taking beech
a leaf whose earnest self-denial fuses digits

into a single arrowhead   unlike both its fig
neighbour's splayed hand soaking up summer sun   and the still
more indolent Japanese maple's plump fingers   less

      sky-aspiring than the veined broadleaf hawthorn's stacked Vs
for victory in the race towards autumn   or the clenched
      red fist of Norway maple   all those leaves more upbeat

      than the last page's weeping willow   thin yellowed hand
    seen sideways   sickle-shaped silhouette reminding her
of an aged actress bowing as the applause fades.

La Mortella

1.

Both trundled their childhoods with them into the garden,
   hers the lighter burden partly because more recent
      (childhood taking on greater weight with distance), partly

because of the hummingbirds young Susana had freed
   from trumpet flowers that imprisoned them each twilight
      at home in Buenos Aires, whir of wings then lifting

her heart as her fingers would lift silk-tree seedpods from
   an Argentine arbour and plant them in Mortella.
      His childhood, arid as the mill chimneys of Oldham,

and shadowed by his father's nearly drinking away
   the fare for a scholarship test young William nearly
      missed, made later life a quest for the light and water

2.

Susana's garden holds. Here, unhindered sun plays off
   the sea-green hummingbirds' thousand-mirrored throats, and he—
      the composer with an ear so keen piano keys

blared like trumpets unless muffled—breathed in the scent-notes
   that silently crescendo along steep terraced rows
      where buckthorn arranges leaves in alternating turns

like his-and-hers or tick-and-tock, in a place that weds
   flower to flow and that measures out through its fountains
      the hours that spell themselves as sky-blue blossoming thyme.

Winter Flowers

on the least sunlit days   starburst of white petals from
dark leathery leaves   no wonder black hellebore picked
up its nickname of Christmas Rose   no wonder Frances

picked it as her favourite flower   determined to bloom
from cold loam in the face of bitter east winds   plucky
as wrens and woodpeckers combing the bark of leafless

beeches   at this *best season* for glimpsing symmetries
unique to every species   with branch and spray unmasked
by foliage   the only time to gather blossoms

from elm   ash   and the willows whose rich yellow plumage
of catkins the blind patients would finger and liken
to velvet   amazed to learn by touching that willows

flowered   their sense of touch more sapient and nimble
than hands of the sighted   so with sweet bay or lilac
their reflexes grew keener to savour the perfumes

as if their darkened eyes let fingers and nostrils come
closer to the source   the way a Christmas Rose quickens
to brightness in the long nights of December's doldrums

and as if the source of light were no celestial flame
but a blaze at the Earth's core   inscribing epistles
on air with fragrance and on petal and leaf in braille.

Sonnets to Orpheus, 1:14

from the German of Rainer Maria Rilke

We go round with flower, vine-leaf, fruit.
They speak not just the language of a year.
From the darkness, a bright unfurling rises,
tinged perhaps with hues of resentment

from the dead who invigorate the earth.
What do we know of their share in that?
From long ago, it has been their part
to imbue the loam with their unanchored pith.

Now we ask: do they willingly do it?
Does this fruit, the work of downcast slaves,
thrust up a fist to us—to their masters?

Are *they* the masters, who sleep among the roots
and grant us, from their superfluity,
this in-between state of mute strength and kisses?

V

Outreachings:
"a creativity we cannot fathom"

Brushpower

The smallest painting

when placed on a wall   opens

a doorway through it

Bridging

1. Paul Cézanne, *Le Pont de Maincy*, 1879-80

You can cross Cézanne's bridge even though the wooden span
gave way to steel a lifetime ago   and even though
it bridges the Almont at Trois Moulins   nowhere near

Maincy   and even though its left end perches on air
like a diving board   remote from the stone pier that sits
distantly behind it   you can cross it not by foot

but by eye   and not from right to left but from the gap
of sky glimpsed through dense leaf-squiggles over the bridge rail
straight back towards you out of the picture onto the wall

of your retina   Cézanne's canvas bridging the scene
he painted and the fovea's imaging   to frame
the interplay between his brushstrokes and the viewer's

vision   in all its tandemness   the landscape we shape
from his shapings   shimmer-patches   clusters   stacks   and from
his knowing we never step twice onto the same bridge.

2. Richard Estes, *Citarella Fish*, 1991

A vertical metal strip on the building's corner
could be the harpoon Ahab flung as he lunged to kill
the messenger from the deep   but here the deep opens

beside not beneath   calm sea of plate glass the chrome strip
edges   a bridgehead holding the realm of fishes back
except that the dark interior has poured shadow

over the pavement on this side of the street   the way
seepage darkens a beach on the waves' flank   from the sole
spot of sun a blue-shirted man uses a payphone

perhaps to talk to his mirrored image far within
the glass   a dangerous place hedged in by body parts
of dead fish in the window display   and menaced by

neon ice floes overhead   where finned cabs run red lights
and where   from under the spar of a backwards sign   comes
the charging baleen of a truck's radiator grille.

3. Robert Lemay, *Two Pears and Old Books*, 2010

The three stacked books bridge a void   nothing below to show
what they rest on or over   no pier-shadow   no gleam
of current   though the leather spines themselves are guttered

and eddied from the spillage of time   like the crumbling
stucco of medieval bridges   making the two pears
atop the books look newborn   their skins radiant with

promise of sweetness   the white inside them still uncut
and printless   unlike the book's pages   yet their savour
will not outlast leather's musty taint   the right-hand one

already age-spotted and branded with the shadow
of its greener partner's stem   while the books' leaves   water-
marked and foxed   will go on whispering secrets into

the future's ear   a spooling seasonal yield compassed
by the tree bark of bindings   the rows of print bridging
the space between one islanded voice and another.

Liberation

still eludes them both after de Gaulle's Free French have marched
in triumph down the Champs-Élysées   she sits boxed in
by tall pilasters and the brass bar of a news rack

above her head at Deux Magots   his box the black one
that lets in for a fraction of a second the light
filtered through gauze curtains whose meander-stitched border

must uncomfortably recall the occupation's
spidering swastikas   although neither Doisneau nor
de Beauvoir owe their confinement to the Nazis   he

a love-starved orphan so locked in shyness that at first
he trains his lens on pavement   raising it degree by
slow degree to children's faces and then adults'   she

in a man's France locked in a woman's body subject
to monthly invasion   her hands not manacled but
ghostwriting Jean-Paul Sartre's journalism to leave him

free to concentrate on his own creative writing
while hers serves time   both de Beauvoir and Doisneau finding
in time the freedom Liberation Day denied them

by making it themselves   he posing and framing life
as I would like it to be   she writing a new world
where *the human couple will discover its true form.*

A Handful of Loam

The uprising that begins down among the roots and rhizomes is first of all a transformation of perception.
— Des Kennedy, Canadian gardener and environmentalist

Beyond, not above, beneath the eye's reach,
the nether-other world where we were born
flowers in darkness. In a single year
of an acre's life, plowing earthworms turn

eighteen tons of loam. Mycelial threads
finer than any silkworm's spinnings wind
for hundreds of miles in a thimbleful
of soil. Molecules of sugar, siphoned

down through a maple's branches, trunk, and root,
sweeten the spicebush where a swallowtail
stokes up, and earth the gardener's cupped hand scoops
throngs with more living beings than the globe

holds people. His unaided eye cannot
take in this plenty, but his lips smile with
the sweetness as he sees a fresh-hoed plot's
furrows redrawn small in his fingerprints,

or a cousin of the pear's mottled skin
sheathing the hand that picked the fruit. Some sense
beneath his senses joys in the twinship
of cellmates at the soil's heart and inside

his own, those microscopic lives that run
our marathon. He knows, however much
they look like two, husband and wife, his flesh
and the pear's flesh under the skin are one.

A Dance of Life

The heels you sway on here are those of the hands   while feet
stand firmly anchored unless the music works its way
down through your body   and the gentle rocking movement

loosens knotted bones into the grace of waterweeds
dreaming on the current's pulse   calm in the in-and-out
of palms and fingers as they push and fold back the dough

on the floured board   turning it over on itself
like sea-waves engaged in the non-stop marathon dance
that first brought life to the land   and now your hands respond

to the life within this partner   moment by moment
less clay than spirited flesh   perfuming the room's air
with the yeast-scent of the sea   which becomes one with you

when you inhale   and if   after your hands have rounded
and stroked the shoulder of the loaf   you kiss your fingers
they'll taste sweet   though not with the sustaining sweetness that

in the afterlife of the dough   beyond the dark warmth
and the rising   your tongue will know when it dances
through the hundreds of oval-domed sea caves in new bread.

First-Hand

carries him beyond clock hands   well past the sweep that flicks
seconds aside quick as a swift's wingbeat   farther back
than the minute-hand against whose ticks he measures out

the cricket's summer song   deeper in time than even
Timothy the tortoise burrowing into earth with
motion *little exceeding the hour-hand*   time layered

like freestone lining the sunken cart lanes with traces
of past lives   rootbreak or coach track hoofprint   charactered
script unveiled but not perceptible *to indifferent*

observers   White himself hardly indifferent   incensed
by the hedge-cuckoo's sleight-of-egg   *a monstrous outrage
on maternal affection*   and moved when   *gaping for*

breath   parenting flycatchers hover above the nest
to shield their featherless brood from scorching noons   he feels
one with the so-called lower forms of life   close watching

wakes him   to the wonder of thumb-sized migrants guided
by instinct across continents where reason stumbles
or to an elegant perfect circle suspended

in the head of a thistle   the *procreant cradle*
of a nest containing *eight little mice . . . naked and
blind*   akin in their helplessness to the field-crickets

that *expressed distress* when *taken out of their knowledge
never stirring but a few inches* from their holes   like
Gilbert White long unstirred from Selborne   so like and so

unlike   one life taking its time through seven decades
another unreeling *with the inconceivable*
swiftness of a meteor   born with head too heavy

for its neck to support   and yet within a fortnight
scaling sea-clouds   as if the eternal clockmaker
allotted each creature a single round   but set one

tortoising along the moon's circuit graved on the face
of the timepiece   and thrust another inscrutably
inside the works onto the flywheel   whirling then gone

Ellwanger's Travels

Call him the first space explorer   if space flight involves
leaving the eye's plain sights to rove an unseen terrain
known only to the scouting expeditions of ear

or nose   tracing the untreadable paths of soundwaves
through dense cedar groves to their source in a crow's solo
or the three-way conversation of river   pebbles

and alder leaves   and penetrating the undergrowth
on grasshopper-thin fluting from *shy and evasive*
yellow-winged sparrows   a hushed *grace-note in the ceaseless*

orchestration of the midsummer fields   which also
pipe their music along scent-highways   fragrance being
the voice of a flower   whether it follows lines scored

for a massed choir of alfalfa   or light airs transposed
to a violet's keen treble   siren-song stronger than
mere characteristics of form or colour to lift

a listener's body from its confines in the dark cold
of a Rochester winter   as one clove of garlic
bears *all Italy* in its *fine penetrating smell*

and a Strasbourg pâté has the power to *summon*
verdant meads of the Alsace plain and *soft contours of*
the Vosges outlined against the distant sky while a cork

frees *all that is sunshine* from Médoc   outer spaces
drawn into the head's resounding and redolent caves
and brought within reach of the mind's intangible hands.

Wolf Hat Traps the Moon

as Raven beak grips the sun   Preston Singletary's
blown glass hat holding light more slyly   in keeping with
the ice-illumined night's slippery disc   the flat round brim

of this upended bonnet porous   catching a spot-
light beam only to focus and spread it on the plinth
like a filleted fish   each side half-circling the crown

with shadow-sculpted snout   teeth   paws   in transformation
to shapes more owl-eyed or more flippered   as glass itself
never settles   shifting solid liquid on its way

from microcrystal birth to the inevitable
shattering-back   yet earning   by passage through a fire
like the self-burning Copper River flames that breathed life

in the Tlingit story   current of light for a while
through its frail breath-formed frame   no spruce hat rooted in earth
but an ear cupped to catch the spilled wolf-call of the moon.

O

not the open hellmouth of a scream   not the silent
pearl's closed circle   this wordless O the potter tosses
hand to hand   spins on her wheel into a cylinder

as the treadle wheel of Earth draws us all into fit
vessels for the ever-spillable   this O   endowed
with innerness   will   when caught in a kiln on the path

from clay to glass   hold its pose midway between bricky thick
and airy not-there   porcelain   wall of white that light
sees through   all flesh's effort to escape its muddy

beginnings and bleach itself to sheerest angel-wing
fulfilled in an O   the stilled wave of its contour   but
O   not now   now she embraces its changes   her hands

engaged in kinetic conversation with the jug's
moist lip   her fingers like a barn swallow's wings dipping
and banking in answer to the unvoiced consonants

of curve and glide   navigating with tactile insight
the flux's momentary affirmations   before
slow drying and kiln fire freeze its rapids   yet even

then the white messenger will keep speaking to other
hands   telling them by feel where her thumbnail notched the rim
in sign language   a breakable annunciation

Hand-Me-Downs

There it was, word for word,
The poem that took the place of a mountain.
He breathed its oxygen,
Even when the book lay turned in the dust of his table.
                    —Wallace Stevens

Where were the birds? His poem was a garden,
lined up in neat rows on the raked white ground,
and at the end of every row, a flower
leaned artfully across to touch its neighbour.
But no tree swallows ringed the stanza yards
with song, no mourning doves stood guard
in tailcoats along furrows where
no robins pecked for worms. The windless air
left petals unruffled. Silence lay unheard.
There it was, word for word,

but the letters embraced only each other: none
climbed out of its black jacket towards the sun
or lifted serif-nectaries to release
sweetness—not to be gathered by the *b*'s,
which could take flight no more than *c*'s could in-
undate his margins. If no amount of brooding
hatched fresh-inked *w*'s that fluttered
minuscule wings deft as a butterfly
freed from its chrysalis, who could pen
a poem that took the place of a mountain?

He took a deep breath that flung out a word—
unprintable. In its fricatives he heard
the same rough music made by lips and tongues
long stilled: the utterly-present air his lungs
had hugged soared into the world on pinions
fledged in the past. Words were not, then,
sunlit morning glories or
afternoons, but black arrangements, scored
notations waiting for the future and the person
who breathed its oxygen.

Like a bat at nightfall setting out to forage,
her voice would ring down the long corridors,
test by soundings the length of shaft, the distance
from the dark cave wall. By instinct she would sense
each turn of line, the poem's vocables
guiding her along still traceable
paths of his soul. Although the hand
that set them down had gone, the words remained
alive, their music uncontainable
even when the book lay turned in the dust of his table.

Notes

"Decipherings": Beginning at age eleven, Mary Anning (1799–1847), self-taught paleontologist who survived being struck by lightning as an infant just after her older sister and namesake had perished in a fire, discovered and reassembled some of the world's most important fossil finds.

"Lotte Reiniger's Magic Shadows": Lotte Reiniger (1899–1981) invented silhouette animation, cutting out shadow figures and sets for silent films (*The Adventures of Prince Achmed*, *Papageno*) and for her many short features based on Grimm's fairy tales.

"Thoreau's Pencils": While working at John Thoreau & Co. (makers of "new and superior" pencils), Henry David Thoreau introduced many innovations and found by experiment that increasing the amount of clay in a pencil produced a harder lead.

"'Bird's Nest' Hunt": Physically challenged to the point of near-immobility, still-life painter William Henry Hunt (1790–1864) was known as "Bird's Nest" Hunt because of his extraordinary skill in depicting such detailed objects.

"The Zeeland Tapestries": A set of six tapestries, woven between 1593 and 1600, the Zeeland Tapestries depict crucial battles in the Netherlands' first struggle for independence from Spain, 1572–76.

"Confinements": What little we know of Lawrence Mocha may be found in Darby Penney and Peter Stastny's *The Lives They Left Behind: Suitcases from a State Hospital Attic* (New York: Bellevue Literary

Press, 2009). The story of Genie (a pseudonym) has been documented in Russ Rymer's *Genie: A Scientific Tragedy* (New York: HarperPerennial, 1994).

"Keys for the Homeless": Pianist Alice Herz-Sommer (1903–2014) kept herself and her young son alive by giving recitals at the Theresienstadt concentration camp, performing works by Bach, Beethoven, Schumann, and Chopin. She had learned all twenty-four Chopin Études by heart; her fellow inmates found Op. 10, No. 12 and Op. 25, No. 1 particularly moving.

"Needlework from the English Civil War": Elizabeth Isham (1609 –1654), needleworker and herbalist, created both an extended autobiographical narrative and an artifact consisting of a sheet of paper folded into small squares, each documenting a year of her life in minute and allusive fragments of writing, which the first part of this poem tries to capture.

"Transparencies": A decade after being photographed by Lewis Carroll, Alice Liddell posed as Cordelia for the photographer Julia Margaret Cameron, in a print later owned by Maurice Sendak.

"La Mortella": On the Italian island of Ischia, La Mortella ("place of myrtles") was the home of English composer William Walton and his Argentine wife Susana, who turned a rocky hillside and valley into a fountain-fed tropical and Mediterranean garden.

"Winter Flowers": Frances Jane Hope (1822–1880) grew flowers for the sick, the poor, and the blind in Edinburgh. Her lively, observant essays appeared in *Notes and Thoughts on Gardens and Woodlands* (1881).

"Liberation": Before he became known for his photograph of *The Kiss*, Robert Doisneau took Simone de Beauvoir's photo in 1945, before she wrote *The Second Sex*.

"First-Hand": Gilbert White (1720–1793) has become known as the first ecologist. Close observation of nature characterized his life and found fullest expression in *The Natural History of Selborne,* from which the italicized phrases are taken.

"Ellwanger's Travels": George Herman Ellwanger (1848–1906) grew up in his family's nursery business in Rochester, New York, and wrote on Gilbert White, gardens, and cuisine; italicized phrases are from *Idyllists of the Country Side, The Garden's Story,* and *Pleasures of the Table.*

Acknowledgements

This book began almost a decade ago, when Ágnes Cserháti invited me to write some ekphrastic poems about her father Péter Cserháti's artwork for a forthcoming catalogue of his carvings, sketches, and paintings. My subsequent conversations with Péter and my creative response to his art culminated in a number of poems included in *Péter Cserháti—Hidden Treasures in Woodcarving, Sculpture, and Sketches: Ekphrastic Poems by John Reibetanz* (Toronto: Rufus Books, 2012). They also prompted me to reflect more broadly on handiwork of all sorts—from painting, photography, and sculpture to gardening, needlework, and cooking. What creative urges are met and embodied in them? How does each negotiate the relationship between nature and human culture, between the individual and the group? How does the creative impulse confront permanence and change, violence and what George Herbert called "the good fellowship of dust"? And—perhaps the most pressing question—what's the good of it all, what can it do for us?

Some of the resulting poems have appeared in *The Antigonish Review, Audeamus, Epignosis Quarterly, The Fiddlehead, Grain Magazine, The Malahat Review*, and the *Southwest Review*, and a selection of them was shortlisted for the 2015 *Malahat Review* Long Poem Prize: I am grateful to the editors and readers for their continuing encouragement. I am also grateful to Petra Hardt at Suhrkamp Verlag and to Victoria Fox at Farrar, Straus and Giroux for permission to publish my translation of Durs Grünbein's "Mantegna vielleicht," from *Nach den Satiren*, subsequently published in the dual-language *Ashes for Breakfast* (Farrar, Straus and Giroux, 2005).

I have benefited enormously from conversations—some fleeting, others over decades—with expert practitioners of various kinds of handiwork, picking up a fuller sense of what it's like to be looking out from inside such arts and crafts as carving, painting, photography, needlework, and gardening. I want here to record my gratitude to Jane Atkins, Alfredo Barutti, Holly Briesmaster, Marlene Creates, Péter Cserháti, the late Betty How, the late Robert Kemp, Robert Lemay, Carla Nagle, and Irvin Rubincam, and to the many others whose names may have escaped the grasp of memory but whose practice has contributed to mine.

Once again, I want to thank the members of the Vic writing group for their patience, critical acumen, and kindness; this time I owe a particularly large debt to Allan Briesmaster, Maureen Hynes, Ruth Roach Pierson, and Leif Vaage. I also owe much to the friendship and continued interest of John Barton, Barry Dempster, Jeffery Donaldson, Richard Greene, Ross Leckie, and Al Moritz. At Brick Books, my good friend and fellow poet Sue Chenette has been an extraordinary editor—meticulous and tenacious, enthusiastic and inspired. Also at Brick, I am very grateful to Alayna Munce for the care and generosity shown throughout the process of turning the manuscript into a book. Most of all, my wife Julie continues to offer unstinting support, keen judgment, and heartfelt encouragement for every piece of work that comes from this lucky practitioner's hand.

John Reibetanz is the author of eleven previous collections of poetry, and his poems have appeared in such magazines as *Poetry* (Chicago), *The Paris Review*, *The Walrus*, and *Canadian Literature*. A finalist for the National Magazine Awards, the National Poetry Competition, and the ReLit Award, John has given readings in major cities all across Canada. He lives in Toronto and is a Senior Fellow at Massey College and a Fellow of Victoria College, where he received the first Victoria University Teaching Award. *The Essential John Reibetanz*, edited by Jeffery Donaldson, was published by The Porcupine's Quill in 2017.